P9-BVG-742

THE LOVE LETTERS OF HENRY VIII

King Henry at the age of forty-nine, four years after the death of Anne Boleyn. He is dressed in the splendid clothes made for his marriage to Anne of Cleves.

Henry was the first English king to be educated as a Renaissance prince and his love for learning and art was combined with an equally strong love of splendour and show.

From the Royal Academy of Arts, London.

the
LOVE
LETTERS
of
HENRY VIII

EDITED AND WITH
A NEW INTRODUCTION
BY

Jasper Ridley

CASSELL

First published in the UK 1988 by Cassell plc,
Artillery House, Artillery Row, London SW1P 1RT

This edition copyright © Cassell 1988
Introduction copyright © Jasper Ridley 1988

British Library Cataloguing in Publication Data
Henry, *VIII, King of England*
    The love letters of Henry the Eighth.
    1. England. Henry VIII, King of England.
    I. Title   II. Ridley, Jasper, *1920–*
942.05'2'0924

ISBN 0 304 23313 X

Typeset by August Filmsetting in Poliphilus

Printed in Great Britain
at the University Printing House, Oxford
by David Stanford
Printer to the University

CONTENTS

Prince Arthur, eldest son of Henry VII, was Catherine of Aragon's first husband. Following the marriage Arthur wrote to his parents-in-law, Ferdinand of Aragon and Isabella of Castile, and assured them that he would be a good husband. Arthur and Catherine arrived at Ludlow Castle early in the new year of 1502 to begin married life: by April Arthur was dead.

Henry's wife, Elisabeth, died following childbirth shortly after Arthur's death and the King considered marrying Catherine himself. Queen Isabella of Castile objected strongly and so it was agreed that Prince Henry should become her new husband.

Portrait from the Royal Collection.

THE WIVES OF HENRY VIII

CATHERINE OF ARAGON

Born 1485. Married Arthur, prince of Wales on 14 November 1501. Widowed 2 April 1502. Married Henry, King of England in 1509. Divorced 1533. Died 7 January 1536.

ANNE BOLEYN

Born c 1501. Married Henry VIII January 1533. Marriage declared valid by Cranmer in May 1533. Crowned Queen 1 June 1533. Marriage dissolved 17 May 1536. Beheaded 19 May 1536.

JANE SEYMOUR

Born c 1509. Married Henry VIII 30 May 1536. Died following childbirth 24 October 1537.

ANNE OF CLEVES

Born 1515. Married Henry VIII 6 January 1540. Marriage nullified July 1540. Died 1557.

KATHERINE HOWARD

Born 1521. Married 28 July 1540. Beheaded 13 February 1542.

KATHERINE PARR

Born 1512. Married Henry VIII 12 July 1543. King Henry died 28 January 1547 and Katherine then married Thomas Seymour, uncle of Edward VI and brother of Jane Seymour. Gave birth to Seymour's child 30 August 1548. Died 7 September 1548. Henry VIII was Katherine Parr's third husband. She had previously been married first to Lord Borough and then to Lord Latimer.

INTRODUCTION

The Background

Four hundred and sixty years ago, the seventeen love letters that Henry VIII wrote to Anne Boleyn, now republished here, were an important state secret: they were the object of an act of international espionage, which was so secret and successful, that we now have very little idea as to what really happened. We can only feel grateful to the secret agent, whoever he was, for it is thanks to him that we can read these charming letters today.

It was probably in 1526 that Henry VIII first fell in love with Anne Boleyn. He was thirty-five, and she was probably about twenty-five, for it is more likely that she was born about 1501 than in 1507, as was formerly believed. He had been King of England for seventeen years. Seven weeks after his accession, and a fortnight before his eighteenth birthday, he had married his brother's widow, Catherine of Aragon. She was six years older than he.

He was still handsome and vigorous in 1526, 6 ft 4 in tall, broad-shouldered, his red hair worn long on to his collar, and clean-shaven. He was both an intellectual and an athlete. He played the lute and composed music, was a great jouster in tournaments, and an excellent archer with the longbow at the butts. He had a great appetite for food and drink. He spent much time in hunting, sometimes riding thirty miles in pursuit of stags, though he still found time to attend mass five times a day, for he was a pious orthodox catholic. Already he was a cold, calculating, and ruthless statesman. He took rapid decisions, but disliked the routine work of government, which he left to his counsellors, especially to Cardinal Wolsey. He wrote theological books, which he dictated to his secretaries, but disliked the physical effort of writing with his own hand. This may be one of the reasons why his love letters to Anne Boleyn are short.

As a young man he had mistresses, though fewer than most of the other kings in Europe. We know for certain of only two love affairs before he fell in love with Anne Boleyn: one was with a lady at his court, Elizabeth Blount, who bore him an illegitimate son in 1519; the second was with Anne's elder sister, Mary Boleyn.

The Boleyns were a family of Norfolk gentry, who had moved to Hever in Kent at the end of the fifteenth century. Anne's father, Thomas, married the daughter of the Duke of Norfolk, was knighted, and became a prominent courtier, soldier, and diplomat. He served as ambassador in France and Spain. In 1525 he was raised to the peerage, with the title of Viscount Rochford, and in 1529 was created Earl of Wiltshire. Only this last advancement could conceivably have been due to Anne's relations with the King.

9

He sent his daughter, Anne, to be educated at the courts of Margaret, the Regent of the Netherlands, and of King François I of France. Mary Boleyn had also been sent to the French court, where she quickly adapted herself to the immoral atmosphere there. François stated later that she had been the most promiscuous lady at his court, which was certainly saying something, for his court had the reputation of being the most immoral in Europe. Soon after Mary returned to England, she became Henry VIII's mistress, and when she married William Carey – a gentleman of the court – in 1520, the King attended the wedding. He afterwards knighted Carey, and gave him gifts of land.

Anne, unlike her sister, did not become notorious at the French court. She was always much harder to win than Mary, either through calculation or from instinct.

Anne seems to have been one of those girls who, according to her enemies and to most other women, was not beautiful or even moderately good-looking, but was very attractive to men. They were always falling in love with her. This is a tribute to her personality, for in the sixteenth century, when men had rather conventional views about women's beauty, Anne did not comply with the prevailing ideas. To judge by all the poets and ballad singers, men liked women to be fair, with golden hair. Women with black or brown hair appear only as villainesses in the romances and ballads. Anne had a swarthy complexion, and though her hair was dark, she was proud of it, sometimes letting it flow loosely over her shoulders. In her portrait she appears witty and intelligent, with the kind of looks that, in the sixteenth century, pleased Frenchmen more than English-men. She was also high-spirited and even domineering, in an age when women were expected to be demure and submissive.

When she returned from France and came to Henry's court, Henry Percy, the Earl of Northumberland's son, fell in love with her, and she with him. They wished to marry, but Cardinal Wolsey prevented this as he had other matri-monial plans for them both. According to Wolsey's usher, George Cavendish, Anne never forgave Wolsey for this, and when she had secured her influence over Henry, she determined to ruin Wolsey, and succeeded in doing so. When Wolsey fell from power, nearly everyone believed that it was Anne's doing. This is certainly not disproved by the fact that she sometimes wrote him charming letters (see her two letters to him on pp. 69, 71, written in June and July 1528), and continued to do so even after his fall a year later.

Sir Thomas Wyatt, the courtier, diplomat and poet, fell in love with Anne. According to Wyatt's grandson, she had a protruding nail between two of the fingers of her right hand. This small excrescence was doubtless the origin of the story told by her catholic enemies that she had six fingers on one hand.

The legal and theological issues involved in Henry's divorce from Catherine of Aragon, and the slow development of the long divorce proceedings, are described in Oldys' Introduction to Henry's love letters, published in the *Harleian Miscellany* in 1745, and reprinted here (see pp. 21–28). Oldys' account contains many errors, and was written with the strong bias of an eighteenth-century English protestant. It is clear that, by the spring of 1527, three factors had made Henry wish to obtain an annulment of his marriage to Catherine: his anxiety about having no legitimate son and his belief that God had condemned his marriage; his repudiation of his alliance with Catherine's nephew, the Holy Roman Emperor, Charles V; and his passionate love for Anne Boleyn. The letters he wrote to Anne at this time (Letters I, II, IV, V, VIII, and X) show the depth of his feelings for her. Anne, unlike her sister, Mary, was refusing to become his mistress — in the modern sense of that word — for when a sixteenth-century gentleman referred to a lady as his mistress (as Henry does in these letters to Anne) he might mean no more than a woman with whom he was deeply in love, and whom he wished to serve and obey as a servant serves and obeys a mistress. When Henry describes himself in the letters as Anne's 'servant', he is using the word, as it was so often used by his contemporaries (in contrast to 'mistress') to mean a man who is in love with a woman.

In the summer of 1528 there was an outbreak of the dreaded sweating sickness, which first came to England in 1485 and frequently returned during the next sixty-five years, until it disappeared after the last visitation in 1551. It seems to have been a very violent form of influenza; the victims fell ill, very suddenly, with a high temperature, and either died or recovered almost completely within forty-eight hours. Henry was always very nervous of catching 'the sweat', partly because he knew that a civil war would probably break out in England if he died before he had produced a male heir. When he learned that a servant of Anne Boleyn's had caught the sweat, he reluctantly decided to send Anne away from court to prevent her from infecting him, and she went to her father's house at Hever. Henry went to his house at Waltham, but when some of his courtiers and servants caught the sweat there, he moved to another of his houses at Hunsdon, where he took refuge in a tower with no one in attendance except one or two grooms of his Privy Chamber. He was afraid that Anne would catch the infection that had appeared in her household, and while he was at Hunsdon he heard, to his dismay, that she had indeed caught the sweat at Hever; but she quickly recovered. His three letters to her at this time (Letters IX, III, and XII) were all written from Hunsdon, in this order, at intervals of a few days between 16 and 23 June 1528.

At last, after a delay of more than a year, the Pope agreed to send Cardinal Campeggio to England to sit with Wolsey on a court that could grant Henry his divorce. In September 1528, Henry heard with joy that Campeggio had reached Paris (see Letter VI), and by 7 October he had arrived in Southwark; but he was still unable to take steps to further the divorce because he was ill with gout. Henry was confident at this time that the delay would only be temporary (see Letter XVII – the last, chronologically, of his surviving letters to Anne), but he and Anne were to be disappointed again. There was a further delay of eight months before the divorce hearing began; and in July 1529, having received new instruc-tions from Rome, Campeggio adjourned the court indefinitely, without giving judgment in Henry's favour.

After two more years had elapsed, Henry separated from Catherine, and began to cohabit openly with Anne. It was probably at this time, in 1531, that she first agreed to go to bed with him. In January 1533 Henry learned that Anne was pregnant, and might, perhaps, be carrying a son who would be the long-awaited male heir to the throne if he married Anne before the baby was born. They were married about 25 January 1533. He instructed Parliament to pass an Act forbidding appeals from the English courts to Rome. After appointing Anne's chaplain, Cranmer, as Archbishop of Canterbury, he arranged for Cranmer to try the divorce case and give judgment that Henry and Catherine had never been lawfully married. It was then announced that Henry and Anne were husband and wife, and on Whit Sunday, 1 June 1533, she was crowned at Westminster as Queen of England.

Her child, who was born on 7 September, was not a son but a daughter, who later became Queen Elizabeth I. During the next three years, Anne became pregnant several times, but always miscarried. Henry decided to rid himself of Anne. She seemed unable to give him a male heir; his minister, Thomas Crom-well, wished to make an alliance with Charles V, whose ambassador made it plain that this could not happen as long as Henry was married to Anne; and Henry had fallen in love with Jane Seymour, one of Anne's ladies-in-waiting.

On 2 May 1536 Anne was arrested and sent to the Tower on a charge of high treason. She was accused of committing adultery with five men, including her brother, and of plotting with them to assassinate Henry. She and her alleged lovers were tried and found guilty, though the charges were almost certainly false. The men were all executed on 17 May. Two days later, Anne was beheaded, but not before Cranmer had divorced her from Henry on the grounds that their marriage had been void, as Henry had previously had intercourse with her sister, Mary – though the grounds for the divorce were kept secret. The result of this judgment was to bastardise Elizabeth, and to clear the way for the future children of Henry and Jane Seymour, whom Henry married a few days after Anne's execution.

The Letters

The seventeen letters published here were probably the only letters from Henry to Anne, for usually she was at court, and he wrote to her only when she was at Hever. We know from the letters that she also wrote to him, but none of her replies have survived. Henry probably destroyed them, considering them to be too compromising, for he was always cool and calculating, even when he was in love. She kept his letters, perhaps because she realised that they could give her a hold over him, or perhaps only for the reasons that women wish to keep letters from their lovers.

Nine of the seventeen letters, and all those written before the end of 1527, are in French. Henry, like all princes, was brought up as a child to speak and to write French, and regularly spoke French with the foreign ambassadors at his court. Anne, having spent some years at the French court, was equally at home in the language. Henry doubtless wrote to her in French as a security precaution. Though princes and diplomats spoke French, most English ladies and gentlemen did not, and very few servants understood French. If Henry's letters to Anne had fallen into the hands of anyone at Hever, no one there would have been able to read them except Anne's father, and perhaps also her mother and the chaplain. By the summer of 1528, when Henry's interest in Anne was hardly concealed, there was much less need for such precautions, and nearly all his letters to her at this time were written in English.

What happened to the letters? All that we know for certain is that by the second half of the seventeenth century they were in the Vatican archives in Rome. At that time, when protestants were being persecuted in France and catholics were being persecuted in England, the divorce of Catherine of Aragon and the Reformation of Henry VIII's reign were not yet history – they were still politics.

Catholics were delighted to exhibit the letters to show that Henry had divorced
Catherine, and repudiated the papal supremacy, not (as he had always main-
tained) because he had conscientious scruples about the legality of his marriage,
but because he was consumed with a sinful lust for Anne Boleyn. The first
reaction of English protestants was to denounce the letters as forgeries; but when
Gilbert Burnet, the staunchly protestant bishop, politician, and historian, was
shown the letters in Rome in 1685, he was forced, reluctantly, to admit they were
undoubtedly genuine.

The papal authorities were quite prepared to allow Dr Fall, the Precentor of
York Cathedral, to take copies of the letters in 1682, and in 1714 they were
published in London by the printer, Churchill, in the original French and
English, with an English translation of the French letters. The English protestants had now changed their line about the letters, and argued that they showed
that Henry wished to make Anne his wife, and not his mistress. The editor of the
1714 edition, who was probably the historian, Thomas Hearne, wrote in his
Introduction that the letters

> may serve to convince the Reader, with how little reason the Papists insult us upon
> that Subject [Henry VIII's divorce]. The Writer of this Preface has been a
> Witness of one Instance of this Raillery, which is their shewing these letters at Rome
> to the English as the shameful Beginning of our Reformation . . . But all these
> Impotent Attacks need no other Answer than a just Account of the Facts themselves.

Hearne reprinted the letters in 1720. They were published again in 1745 with
the collection of papers of the late Robert Harley, Earl of Oxford, which became
known as the *Harleian Miscellany*. The Introduction (see pp. 21–28) was anony-
mous, but the writer was the historian William Oldys. The letters were published seven times in England between 1745 and 1949, either in the Harleian or
new editions. The 1907 edition of the version in the *Harleian Miscellany*, which
was reprinted in 1933, was the first to give only the English translation of the
French letters, and did not even mention that some of the letters were written in
French. Henry Savage's edition, in 1949, included for the first time a facsimile of
the original letters in the Vatican archives.

After Napoleon's victories in Italy in 1797, the original letters were removed,
with other manuscripts, from the Vatican to Paris. They were restored to the
Vatican in 1815 after Napoleon's defeat at Waterloo, but not before they had
been transcribed, and in 1826 Crapelet published them in Paris. The French
catholic, Crapelet, writing under the restored Bourbon monarchy, took a differ-

Catherine of Aragon had been betrothed at three to Henry VII's elder son Arthur, prince of Wales. Catherine married Arthur in 1501, less than five months before his death.

When Henry VIII succeeded to the throne in 1509 following the death of his father he insisted on marrying his brother Arthur's widow. Henry was seventeen and Catherine, an intelligent and accomplished woman, was twenty-three. Some of his counsellors thought that the marriage was unlawful, but Henry relied on a papal dispensation which permitted it. Twenty years later, he argued that this dispensation was against God's law, and void. It was Henry's desire for Anne Boleyn and his passionate desire for a male heir that eventually persuaded the King to divorce Catherine.

From the National Portrait Gallery, London.

ent view of Henry VIII from Oldys and the English protestants. He commented sadly that whereas

> *We have seen the most humane, the most virtuous, the most religious of Kings* [Louis XVI of France] *die on the scaffold, Henry VIII, that sinister offspring of the stems of the White Rose and the Red Rose, cruel in character, a tyrant over his people and his family, and the destroyer of the religion of his fathers, died in his bed.*

For this present edition I have presented the eight English letters in the original text, but with modernised spellings, and an English translation of the nine French letters. As far as possible I have followed the English translation given in the *Harleian Miscellany*, but I have substituted my own translation where the Harleian translation is wrong, misleading, or so literal as to be almost incomprehensible. I have also included Anne's two letters to Wolsey, and her last letter to Henry, in the form in which they were published in the 1714 edition and in the *Harleian Miscellany*, with a few minor corrections. Oldys' Introduction to the 1745 edition, which is of historical interest today, has also been included.

Anne's last letter to Henry from the Tower is dated 6 May 1536, four days after her arrest and thirteen days before her execution. It is now in the British Library, and was first published by Burnet in 1679. In the nineteenth and twentieth centuries, all the leading historians pronounced it a forgery. The Edwardian scholar, James Gairdner, who was one of the most learned writers on the Reformation period, stated that it was neither in Anne's handwriting nor in her style. No one can challenge his opinion that it is not in her hand, but when he stated that it was not written in her style, he was expressing a personal opinion with which one is entitled to disagree. If he is wrong about the style, the document in the British Library may be an accurate copy by someone else of the letter that Anne did in fact write.

It is certainly not written in the style in which prisoners accused of high treason in the reign of Henry VIII were expected to write, and usually did write, to the King. If Anne wrote this letter, and Henry read it, he would have been outraged. It might, indeed, explain why he not only showed her no mercy, but also why he openly rejoiced over her death in a way that shocked his contemporaries. The letter bears all the marks of Anne's character, of her spirit, her impudence, and her recklessness. No other letter from Anne to Henry from the Tower, begging for mercy in the accepted style, has survived among the state papers, though one would have expected any such letter to have been carefully preserved by Henry's ministers. In view of this, there seems at least a possibility that the letter is genuine, which is a good enough reason for including, and not omitting, this interesting and attractive document.

The order in which Henry's letters to Anne are numbered, which has been followed in nearly all the editions since Churchill's in 1714, was decided quite fortuitously by an unknown archivist in the Vatican in the sixteenth or seven-teenth century. When the letters reached Rome, they were almost certainly in the state in which they were when Henry wrote them and Anne read them, on separate pieces of thin vellum. The Vatican archivist pasted them on to thicker parchment, apparently in an order chosen at random. This is certainly not the order in which they were written, and it is not easy to know what the chronolog-ical order was, as Henry did not date any of the letters. In the case of Letters III, VI, IX, XII, and XVII, the date can be fixed, to within a few days, by references in the text of the letters. In all the other cases, only an approximate date can be given.

How did the letters get to Rome? Oldys, in his Introduction, puts forward the view that appealed to the English in the seventeenth and eighteenth centuries, that they were stolen by a papal spy, and that when Henry's officers searched Cardinal Campeggio's baggage at Dover when he left England in 1529, in breach of his diplomatic immunity, they were looking for the stolen letters. But it seems unlikely that either Campeggio or the Pope would have wished to steal the letters. The Pope's chief object, throughout his seven years' procrastination over the divorce, was to avoid giving any judgment, or taking any action, that could offend either Henry or Charles V, and he succeeded in doing this until at last he reluctantly gave judgment in Catherine's favour, after Henry had repudiated the papal authority. It is very unlikely that he would have risked antagonising Henry in 1529 by stealing the letters.

Charles V's ambassador in London, Eustace Chapuys, is much more likely to have sent an agent to steal them. He was bitterly opposed to the divorce and to Henry and Anne, and we know that he had at least one secret agent amongst Anne's entourage at court. But did he arrange with this agent for the letters to be stolen from Hever, or from Anne's apartments at court? Chapuys wrote at least once a week to Charles or his ministers, sometimes in code, and nearly all his letters have survived. None of them contains any reference, even a veiled one, to the fact that he had stolen the letters, though he made more compromising revelations than this in his reports. It is also rather unlikely that if Charles had obtained the letters from Chapuys, he would have sent them to the Vatican. He did not trust the Pope, for he condemned his attempts to appease Henry. Charles would certainly have told the Pope about the letters, but he is much more likely to have sent him copies than the originals, which he would have retained in Madrid.

It seems on the whole more likely that they were stolen by some freelance adventurer, who hoped to sell them to the Pope, to the emperor, or to the highest bidder. At some time or other, the thief sold them to someone who sent them to the Vatican, perhaps many years later, although by that time the Pope and his followers could not make much use of them. For this reason they never published them, and did not talk about them for nearly a hundred and fifty years.

Three years after Anne and her brother were executed, their father died at Hever. His house there passed to Henry's fourth wife, Anne of Cleves, after Henry had divorced her, but she only visited it occasionally. When she died in Mary's reign, Hever was sold to Mary's ardent catholic counsellor, Sir Edward Waldegrave. After Mary's death, Waldegrave was deprived of all his offices by Elizabeth I, and soon afterwards was arrested for allowing illegal catholic masses to be celebrated at Hever. He was sent to the Tower, where he died in 1581.

Is it possible that Henry's letters to Anne were not stolen in 1529, and that when Campeggio's baggage was searched, the authorities were not looking for the letters but, as Campeggio himself believed, suspected that he was smuggling Wolsey's valuables out of the country; that Henry and Anne and everyone else forgot about the letters, which remained in a chest at Hever; that Waldegrave found them there thirty years later and, realising their importance, gave them, before he was arrested, to one of the catholic priests whom he sheltered at Hever so that the letters could be taken to Rome; and that the authorities in the Vatican never used them for fear of incriminating Waldegrave, now a prisoner in the Tower in London? This might seem a far-fetched explanation, were it not for the fact that letters are sometimes found in desk drawers after having been there for more than thirty years, and that secret state documents are sometimes lost by negligence only to turn up in the most unexpected places.

JASPER RIDLEY

Anne Boleyn was the niece of the Duke of Norfolk through her mother. Her powerful father, Sir Thomas Boleyn, had married into the Howard family. Her elder sister Mary had been the King's mistress and was perhaps responsible for her father being raised to the peerage as Viscount Rochford. Anne replaced Mary in the King's affections but kept him waiting while she refused to become his mistress and demanded recognition as Queen. In 1532, shortly before her marriage to Henry, she was created Lady Marquess of Pembroke in her own right.

Painting on a panel from the National Portrait Gallery, London.

(As Oldys' Introduction is reprinted here only because of its historical interest, his factual inaccuracies have not been corrected. His spelling of names and other words has been preserved. The footnotes come from his Introduction.)

As these letters, with a few reflections on them, may give those that have not leisure to turn over large volumes, just notions of the grounds of King Henry the Eighth's divorce, and arm them against the calumnies of the papists on that subject, I shall give you a faithful copy of them from the originals, now preserved in the Vatican library where they are usually shewn to all strangers, and a true translation of those that were written in French, introducing them with a short view of the most remarkable transactions which preceded, and gave occasion to them. To which end, it may first be observed that, in King Henry the Seventh's time, his eldest son, Prince Arthur, being[1] past fifteen years of age, was married to the Princess Catherine of Spain, who was elder than himself; that they lived together as man and wife for several months, and then, Prince Arthur dying,[2] it was resolved, for reasons of state, that Prince Henry should marry his brother's widow. This was opposed by Warham, archbishop of Canterbury, as absolutely unlawful, but advised by Fox, bishop of Winchester, who thought all difficulties would be removed by a dispensation, from Rome; accordingly a bull was obtained[3] to that effect, and they were married, the prince being yet under age. But Warham had so possessed the king with scruples against this marriage, that, the day[4] on which the prince was of age, he, by his father's order, protested against it, as null and void; and Henry the Seventh, with his dying breath, persisted in charging his son to break it off intirely. However, when Henry the Eighth came to the crown, it was resolved in council, that he should renew his marriage; which was done[5] publickly, and he had several children by the queen, who all died young, except the Lady Mary.[6]

After this there appeared no farther disquiet in the king's mind, nor any sign of an intended divorce, till the year 1524, when Cardinal Wolsey, by his legantine mandate, published a bull of the pope's against those that contracted marriage within the forbidden degrees. This mandate is yet extant in the register of Fisher, bishop of Rochester. What followed makes this justly suspected to have been done, on the king's account. To confirm which suspicion, there is a concurring circumstance, in a letter from Simon Grineus to Bucer, dated September 10, 1531, where he says, The king had declared to him, that he had abstained from Queen Catherine, for seven years, upon scruples of conscience.

[1]November 14, 1501.   [2]April 2, 1502.   [3]December 26, 1503.   [4]June 22, 1505.
[5]June 3, 1509.   [6]Afterwards Queen of England.

However, though the king had scruples at that time, yet he concealed them carefully from the world for some years; and the immediate occasion of their breaking out seems to have been given by the French ambassadors, who came[1] to England to treat of several matters, and particularly of a marriage between the Princess Mary and the French king, or the duke of Orleans, his second son. This alternative was at last agreed,[2] though it remained sometime in suspense, because the president of the parliament of Paris doubted, whether the marriage between the king and her mother, being his brother's wife, were good or no. The bishop of Tarbe made the same objection, and renewed it to the king's ambassadors in France, as appears by King Henry's speech to the mayor and citizens of London, concerning his scruples, where he says, When our ambassadors were last in France, and motion was made that the duke of Orleans should marry our said daughter, one of the chief counsellors to the French king said, It were well done to know whether she be the king of England's lawful daughter, or not; for well known it is, that he begat her on his brother's wife, which is directly contrary to God's law, and his precept. That this counsellor was the bishop of Tarbe, is affirmed by the bishop of Bayonne, in the account he gives of this speech to the court of France, in a letter dated the 27th of November, 1528; yet this very bishop of Tarbe was afterwards advanced to be a cardinal, and was so far from retracting his opinion, that, when he was cardinal of Grandemont, in a letter dated the 27th of March, 1530, he writes to the French court, That he had served the Lord Rochford (Anne Boleyn's father) all he could, and that the pope had three several times said to him in secret, that he wished the marriage had been already made in England, either by the legate's dispensation, or otherwise; provided it was not done by him, nor in diminution of his authority, under pretence of the laws of God. The conduct shews, that it was not religion, but political views, that turned the court of Rome against the king's cause, which they at first plainly favoured. And now as to the arguments by which the king fortified himself in these scruples. These, as he himself owned, were, that he found by the law of Moses, If a man took his brother's wife, they should die childless; this made him reflect on the death of his children, which he now looked on as a curse from God, for that unlawful marriage. He found Thomas Aquinas (whom he chiefly valued of all the casuists) of opinion, That the laws of Leviticus, about the forbidden degrees of marriage, were moral and eternal, such as obliged all christians; and that the pope could only dispense with the laws of the church, but not with the laws of God; and, when the validity of the marriage came afterwards to be thoroughly canvassed, it appears that the whole tradition of the church and the opinions of its doctors were against the marriage.

In the year 1527, before Cardinal Wolsey's journey to France, which he began on the 3rd of July, to promote the king's marriage with the duchess of Alenson, the king's scruples were become publick, as two writers[3] testify almost in the same words: This season, says Hall, began a fame in London, that the king's confessor, the bishop of Lincoln, called Dr Langland, and divers other great clerks, had told the king, that the marriage between him and the Lady Catherine, later wife to his brother, Prince Arthur, was not good, but damnable.

And this suspicion, of the cardinal's going to promote a second match in France, is confirmed[4] by a letter of his, dated Feversham, July the 5th, 1527, where he says, Archbishop Warham had warned him of the great jealousies which Queen Catherine had of his journey. And by another letter, dated August the 1st, 1527, where he labours to satisfy the king, that the pope's dispensation was in itself null and void. All these particulars will be the stronger proofs of the cardinal's intention, when it shall be proved that the cardinal could then have no thoughts of Anne Boleyn, whose father, the Lord Rochford, came over to England from France with the duchess of Alenson's picture to shew it to King Henry; and it was then, in all probability, that Anne Boleyn came over with him; for, though she had been in England in 1522, yet she did not stay long but returned into the service of Claude, queen of France, where she continued till that queen died, which was in 1524, and then went into the duchess of Alenson's service, which she left probably at this time. Soon after her coming into England, she was taken into Queen Catherine's court, where the Lord Piercy courted her, and was upon the point of marrying her had not Cardinal Wolsey, by the king's order, prevented it; and, as the same author assures us, it was not till after the cardinal's return from France, which was on the last day of September, 1527, that the king opened his affection for Anne Boleyn to him.

Why then do the papists pretend to say, that the king would never have had thoughts of a divorce, or scruples against his first marriage, had not his unlawful passion for Mrs Boleyn prompted him to them? Whereas it is plainly proved that the king's scruples were infused in him from his infancy, on the justest grounds; that they were revived in him three years before they were made public, and that they were commonly talked of, and a new match contrived for him to the duchess of Alenson, before Anne Boleyn appeared at court. All which will still appear more clearly in the ensuing letters. But, before I make any remarks on these, I must first give a short account of the king's negotiations at Rome, without which some of them cannot be understood. In the end of 1527, the king solicited the pope for a commission to judge the validity of his marriage with Queen Cath-

[1]March 2, 1527.   [2]April 30, 1527.   [3]Stow, Hall.   [4]Herbert.

erine, which after some time was obtained in a bull, dated the 13th of April, 1528, impowering Cardinal Wolsey, with the archbishop, or any other English bishop to judge the marriage. But this was not made use of; perhaps because it was thought that a stranger ought to be employed, that the proceeding might be more impartial. So a new commission was desired, and obtained, bearing date the 6th of June, in which the cardinals Wolsey and Campegio (an Italian) were appointed joint legates to judge the marriage.

And, to make this the surer, there was a pollicitation (or promise) procured on the 23rd of July, 1528, That the pope would never inhibit or revoke this commission to judge the marriage; and a decretal bull, which contained an absolute decision of the cause, which was only shewn to the king, and Cardinal Wolsey, by Campegio; but all these precautions which were admitted of, when the pope was in a distressed condition, did not restrain his holiness from sending one Campana before the end of the year, to see the decretal bull secretly burnt; and from recalling the legate's commission, and avocating the cause to Rome the next year, when his affairs were more flourishing, and the emperor (who was Queen Catherine's nephew) had granted all his demands.

Now as to the letters themselves. It may be presumed reasonably, that, if there had been anything in them that had reflected on the king's honour, or on Anne Boleyn's, they would certainly have been published by the papists at that very time; for they were in their hands soon after they were written, as appears from this passage in Lord Herbert's History.

'When Cardinal Campegio came to take ship, the searchers, upon pretence he carried either money or letters from England to Rome, ransacked all his coffers, bags, and papers, not without hope, certainly, to recover that decretal bull our king so much longed for. I find also (some relation) that divers love-letters between our king and Mistress Boleyn, being conveyed out of the king's cabinet, were sought for, though in vain; they having been formerly sent to Rome.'

To explain this account, it must be supposed, that they were taken, not out of the king's, but out of Anne Boleyn's cabinet; this is the more probable, because, in fact, they are all letters from the king to her; whereas, if his cabinet had been rifled, her answers to him would have been more likely to be found there.

As to the time in which the king's letters to Anne Boleyn were written, in all probability, it was immediately after her dismission from the court,[1] which was done to silence the clamours of the people on her account; but she was sent away in so abrupt a manner, that she determined to absent herself altogether; which made the king soon repent of his severity, and press her to come back; but this was

[1]Herbert.

not obtained for a long time, nor without great difficulty; as appears by some of the following letters. The time of her dismission was not till May, 1528, for there is a letter extant[1] from Fox to Gardiner, at Rome, dated London, May the 4th, 1528, where he writes, Of his landing at Sandwich, May the 2nd,——His coming that night to Greenwich, where the king lay,——His being commanded to go to Mistress Anne's chamber in the Tilt-yard——And declaring to her their expedition in the king's cause, and their hastening the coming of the legate——To her great rejoicing and comfort——Then came the king, to whom he delivered his letters,——and opened his negotiations——Then he went to the cardinal, etc.

Soon after the date of this letter she was dismissed; for, in the first of the letters that follow, the king makes excuses for the necessity of their being asunder; and, in the second complains of her unwillingness to return to court. In neither of these is a word of the sweating sickness, which raged violently in June; and, of which he speaks in his third letter, as of a thing that had lasted some time, and, of which, he had formed many observations from experience. Between this letter, which seems to have been writ in July, and the sixth, which, mentioning the legate's arrival at Paris, must have been written in the end of September, there are two letters, which, by the earnestness of the business, were plainly written within a few days of one another. Probably, soon after the latter[2] of these were sent by the king, where he expressed how much he was pleased with her answer to his earnest desire in the former,[3] in the heat of his gratitude, he paid a visit to his mistress, in which time they wrote a joint letter to Cardinal Wolsey, which is added in the appendix, where the king expresses his wonder, that he had not yet heard of the legate Campegio's arrival at Paris; which makes it probable this happened in September. The king stayed not long with her after this; for, when she had received the cardinal's answer, she writes a second letter, without mentioning the king's being there; and, again shews impatience to hear of the legate's coming, of which, the king gave her the first news soon after. But,

To return to the fourth letter, which from all these particulars may be supposed to have been written in August; it is the most important in all the collection, for it fixes the time when his affection to Anne Boleyn began. He complains in it, That he had been above a whole year struck with the dart of love, and not yet sure whether he shall fail, or find a place in her heart or affection. Now, by the nature of his complaint, it is visible, that he pleads all the merits that a long attendance could give him, and, therefore, if, instead of a year, he should have called it a year and a half, or two years, he would certainly have done it to make his argument the stronger. It may likewise be probably concluded from the same words, that he

---

[1]Lately in the Earl of Oxford's library, 39, B4.   [2]Letter the fifth.
[3]Letter the fourth.

Mary, daughter of Catherine of Aragon, painted in 1554, the year after she became Queen. Her father was devoted to his 'fair daughter' but, as he told the Lord Mayor of London and a collection of notables at Bridewell Palace in November 1528, 'yet it hath been told us by diverse great clerks, that neither is she our lawful daughter nor her mother our lawful wife'.

Although Mary went down in history as 'Bloody Mary' she was not innately ruthless. After her accession Mary was advised to order the execution of her ill-fated young cousin Lady Jane Grey, who was in line to the throne and who had been declared Queen, following the death of Edward VI. Lady Jane Grey was eventually executed but as Simon Renard, the Imperial ambassador and one of Mary's intimates wrote of Mary, 'She could not be induced to consent that she should die.'

Portrait from the National Portrait Gallery, London.

had not then known her much above half a year; for it would have been an ill compliment in him, to let her understand that he had seen her some time, before he was at all in love with her.

These remarks confirm the account already given, of her coming from France with her father, and, by that means, serve to establish the king's vindication from the scandal thrown on him by the papists, that he had no scruples about his marriage, till he saw Anne Boleyn.

Though it may be here questioned, how the time of any particular letter can be known, since they have no date, and therefore may have been put out of their order. But those, that will read them with any attention, will find a chain of circumstances referred to that plainly show they were laid together by one that knew the order in which they were written, very likely by Anne Boleyn herself; and whoever stole them, as he took them all together, so would be careful no doubt, to keep them in the order he found them in, that the discoveries to be made from them might be the more complete.

It will not be doubted by any that read these letters, that the king's affection to Anne Boleyn was altogther upon honourable terms. There appears no pretension to any favours, but when the legates shall have paved the way. There is but one offence that can be taken at these letters, which is, that there are indecent expressions in them. But this is to be imputed to the simplicity and unpoliteness of that age which allowed too great liberties of that sort; and it must be owned by his enemies, that there are but three or four of these sallies in all the collection, and that there are letters that make much more for the king's piety and virtue, than those irregularities can sully his character.

In the fifth letter he tells her, God can do it, if He pleases; to whom I pray once a day for that end, and hope, that, at length, my prayers will be heard.

In the sixth, I trust shortly to enjoy, what I have so longed for, to God's pleasure, and our both comforts.

In the ninth, praying God, that (and it be His pleasure), to send us shortly togydder. Surely these religious expressions would have been very improper, to make an unlawful passion succeed.

In the thirteenth, speaking of the ill character of one that was proposed to be made abbess of Wilton, he writes, I would not, for all the gold in the world, clog your conscience nor mine, to make her ruler of a house which is of so ungodly demeanour; nor I trust you would not, that, neither for brother nor sister, I should so destrain mine honour or conscience. The whole letter is of an excellent strain, and would have been a very improper exhortation to one against whose virtue he had a design.

The last of the letters mentions the legate's illness as a reason why he had not yet entered upon his office; which shews that the correspondence ended at least in May 1529 when the process began.

There is but one thing after the letters, that it seems very material to add here in the king's defence and that is, the approbation of his cause by the learned men of Europe.

During the trial, Warham and Fisher, who were the advocates for the queen, declared, That they having been lately consulted by the king, etc., had answered, that the king's conscience was disturbed and shaken, not without the weightiest and strongest reasons.[1]

After the legates had trifled some months, and at last, Campegio, under a pretence of the rules of the court of Rome, had adjourned the court for three months; during which time he obtained an avocation from the pope; the king was advised by Cranmer, not to depend longer on the decisions of the see of Rome, but to consult the several universities of Europe, as well as his own, about the validity of his marriage.

One Crook was employed in this negotiation, and he obtained the opinion of almost all the universities[2] whither he went, for the nullity of the marriage; yet he complains in his letters that he was in great straits from the small allowance he had. And, in an original bill of his accounts it appears that he never gave above a few crowns to any that writ on the king's side; whereas the emperor gave a benefice of five hundred ducates to one, and of six hundred crowns to another, that writ for the queen. Yet, though on the one side men were poorly paid for their trouble, and on the other richly rewarded, yet the most eminent men were universally for the king.

It may here be added that Erasmus, whose name was in the greatest esteem at that time, though he could not be prevailed with to write for the king, for fear of the pope and the emperor, in whose dominions he lived; yet he went so far as to give great encomiums of the worth and virtues of Sir Thomas Boleyn, then earl of Wiltshire, in his book, *De Præparatione ad Mortem*, which he dedicates to him; and this was all the approbation that his circumstances made it convenient for him to shew of the king's cause.

On this general consent of the learned in his favour, the king was told he might proceed to a second marriage, the first being of itself null and void; and, accord-ingly, he married Anne Boleyn, the twenty-fifth of January, 1533.[3]

WILLIAM OLDYS

---

[1] Rymer, Tom, XIV.   [2] See Hist. Reform, Part I.   [3] Hist. Reform, Part III.

King Henry aged 35. As a youth Henry had been accounted the most accom⁄
plished prince in Europe, and the early years of his reign as king had been
successful. But by the mid 1520s, when the portrait was painted, the lack of a
male heir for England had begun to prey on the mind of the King.

From a miniature in the Royal Collection.

LETTER FROM ANNE BOLEYN
TO SIR THOMAS BOLEYN

SIR,
I understand by your letter that you wish me [to meet] all honest women when I come to court, and you inform me that the Queen will take the trouble to speak to me. I am greatly looking forward to the prospect of talking with a person so virtuous and honest. This will make me wish more than ever to continue to learn to speak good French, and also especially because you advised me to do so, and I write with my own hand to tell you that I will adhere to this as far as I can. Sir, I beg you to forgive me if my letter is badly written, for I assure you that it, and the spelling, come from my own hand alone, while the others were written by my hand, but Symonnet dictates the letters and stays while I write them myself, so that you should think that I write them. I beg you that this disclosure will not cause you to renounce your wish to help me, because it seems to me that I can rely on this. You can, if it please you, make this plain to me by your words, and make me know for certain that you will still continue to act as a father to me. No ingratitude will emanate from me or prevent me from performing whatever you command, and I promise you that my love is grounded on so firm a basis that nothing will be able to diminish it and put an end to my resolve and promise. I commit myself most humbly to your good favour.

Written at five o'clock by your most humble and most obedient daughter,

ANNA DE BOULLAN

(This undated letter from Anne Boleyn to her father was probably written from the Netherlands in the summer of 1513, when she was aged eleven or twelve. She had been sent to be educated at the court of Margaret of Austria, Duchess of Savoy, who was Regent of the Netherlands for her father, the Holy Roman Emperor Maximilian I. Anne was being taught French by a tutor named Symmonet. The letter is written in French, and is full of the mistakes which were to be expected from a child who was only beginning to learn the language, though these mistakes can only be appreciated if the letter is read in the original by a scholar who is acquainted with sixteenth-century French spelling and phraseology. The 'Queen' to whom Anne refers was Margaret of Austria, who was not in fact a queen, though in view of her position as regent, and the way in which she dominated her court at Brussels and Malines, it is not surprising that the child thought that she was a queen.)

A SONG OF CONSTANCY

Written by Henry VIII

Grene grouth the holy, so doth the ivie
Thow winter's blastys blow never so hye.
As the holy grouth grene and never chaungyth hew
So I am ever hath bene unto my lady trew

Grene grouth the holy, so doth the ivie
Thow winter's blastys blow never so hye.

As the holy grouth grene with ivie all alone
Whose flowerys cannot be seen and grene wode levys be
      gone,
Now unto my lady, promyse to her I make
From all other only to her I me betake.
Adew myne owne lady, adew my specyall
Who hath my hart trewly, be sure, and ever shall.

Grene grouth the holy, so doth the ivie
Thow winter's blastys blow never so hye.

*One of Henry's tutors had been John Skelton, the poet laureate. Henry was
fond of poetry and song, and was an able musician who could play several
instruments.*

33

The beautifully decorated and ornate writing case of King Henry VIII. The King disliked writing and often dictated but could himself write in Latin, French and English.

The case bears the arms of King Henry and his first queen Catherine of Aragon, the daughter of Ferdinand, King of Aragon and Isabella, Queen of Castile.

From the Victoria and Albert Museum, London.

LETTER I

(Translated from the French. Written before July 1527.)

Y MISTRESS[1] AND FRIEND, I and my heart put ourselves in your hands, begging you to recommend them to your favour, and not to let absence lessen your affection to us. For it were a great pity to increase their pain, which absence alone does sufficiently, and more than I could ever have thought; bringing to my mind a point of astronomy, which is, that the farther the days[2] are from us, the farther too is the sun, and yet his heat is the more scorching; so it is with our love, we are at a distance from one another, and yet it keeps its fervency, at least on our[3] side. I hope the like on your part, assuring you that the uneasiness of absence is already too severe for me; and when I think of the continuance of that which I must of necessity suffer, it would seem intolerable to me, were it not for the firm hope I have of your unchangeable affection for me; and now, to put you sometimes in mind of it, and seeing I cannot be present in person with you, I send you the nearest thing to that possible, that is, my picture set in bracelets, with the whole device, which you know already, wishing myself in their place, when it shall please you. This from the hand of your loyal servant and friend

H REX

---

[1]For the meaning of 'mistress', see the Editor's Introduction, p. 11.
[2]The *Harleian Miscellany* has 'Moors' here (a misreading of 'jours') instead of 'days', although – as Burnet points out – this did not make sense.
[3]Henry here wrote '*nostre*', using the royal plural, but meaning himself as opposed to Anne.

Letter II. Written in French, beginning 'To my Mistress, Because the time seems to me very long . . .'
From the Vatican Library, Rome.

LETTER II

(Translated from the French. Written before July 1527.)

O MY MISTRESS.
Because the time seems to me very long, since I have heard from you, or concerning your health, the great affection I have for you has obliged me to send this bearer to be better informed both of your health and pleasure; particularly because, since my last parting from you, I have been told that you have entirely changed the opinion in which I left you, and that you would neither come to court with my lady your mother, nor any other way; which report, if true, I cannot enough wonder at, being persuaded in my own mind that I have never committed any offence against you; and it seems a very small return for the great love I bear you, to be kept at a distance from the person and presence of the woman in the world that I value the most; and if you love me with as much affection as I hope you do, I am sure the distance between our two persons would be a little uneasy to you: though this will not distress the mistress as much as the servant. Consider well, my mistress, how greatly my absence from you grieves me; I hope it is not your will that it should be so; but if I heard for certain that you yourself desired it, I could do no other than complain of my ill fortune, and by degrees abate my great folly; and so, for want of time, I make an end of my uncouth letter, desiring you to give credit to this bearer in what he will tell you from me. Written by the hand of your entire servant

H Rex

[1]Henry is referring here to the sweating sickness.

[2]Henry wrote '*deux verles de chamber*', and the *Harleian Miscellany* kept the French words '*valets de chambre*' in the translation. The two men referred to were the servants who helped Henry to dress and waited on him in his bedroom. Their official name was 'groom of the Privy Chamber', and Henry would have used this term if he had been writing his letter in English.

[3]'*nous nous somes bien reboutes en v̄re meson de hondson*' was translated in the *Harleian Miscellany* as 'we have returned to your house at Hondson'. But Henry, who came to Hunsdon from Waltham, had not 'returned' there, and '*rebouter*' means to set broken limbs. Henry seems to be using the word in a loose sense here. He certainly wrote '*votre maison*', but this must have been a slip of the pen for '*notre maison*', for Henry, not Anne, had a house at Hunsdon.

[4]'*Im   H Rex   muable.*' Henry evidently meant his signature 'H Rex' to be in parentheses, and wrote this reference to his fidelity to Anne around the signature.

LETTER III

(Translated from the French. Written about 20 June 1528, a few days after Letter IX and a few days before Letter XII.)

HE uneasiness, which my doubts about your health caused me, disturbed and frightened me extremely, and I could not have had any quiet unless I had heard for sure. But as you have not yet felt anything, I hope and feel reassured that it will pass you by,[1] as I hope it has passed us by, for when we were at Waltham two ushers, two grooms of the Privy Chamber,[2] your brother and Mr Treasurer fell ill, and are now quite well; and since we have strengthened ourselves with medicines at our house at Hunsdon[3] we have been quite well, without any illness, God be praised; and I think if you would leave those places on the Surrey side, as we did, you could cross without danger. There is another thing which may comfort you, which is, that it is true, as they say, that few or no women have caught this illness; and what is more, no one at our court, and few elsewhere have died of it. This is why I beg you, my entirely beloved, not to be afraid, nor to be too uneasy at our absence. For wherever I am, I am yours, and yet we must sometimes submit to our misfortunes; for whoever will struggle against fate is generally but so much the farther from gaining his end. Wherefore comfort yourself, and take courage, and keep clear of the disease as far as you can, and I hope shortly to make you sing for joy at your recall. No more at present for lack of time, but that I wish you were in my arms, that I might a little dispel your unreasonable thoughts. Written by the hand of him who is, and always will be yours

UN H REX CHANGEABLE[4]

Woodstock Palace where King Henry often stayed on his summer 'progresses'. Anne Boleyn's daughter the Princess Elizabeth was to be kept prisoner there by her half sister Mary, under the strict custody of Sir Henry Bedingfield, following the anti-Spanish Wyatt rebellion. While at Woodstock, Elizabeth used a diamond to cut brief lines of verse upon a window
    'Much suspected of me
    nothing proved can be.'
    Quoth Elizabeth, Prisoner.
Illustration from the Bodleian Library, Oxford.

LETTER IV

(Translated from the French. Written before July 1527.)

Y turning over in my thoughts the contents of your last letters, I have put myself into a great agony, not knowing how to understand them, whether to my disadvantage, as some passages indicate, or to my advantage, as I interpret other passages. I beseech you now, with all my heart, to let me know your whole intention as to the love between us two; for I must of necessity obtain this answer from you, having been, for more than a year, struck with the dart of love, and not yet sure whether I shall fail, or find a place in your heart and affection; and this last point has prevented me recently from naming you my mistress, which would be inappropriate if you do not love me with more than an ordinary affection, as it denotes a special relationship which is far from ordinary. But if it pleases you to play the part of a true, loyal mistress and friend, and to give yourself body and heart to me, who will be, and has been, your most loyal servant (if your rigour does not forbid me), I promise you that not only will you deserve the name, but also that I will take you for my only mistress, casting all others, that are in competition with you, out of my thoughts and affection, and serving only you. I beg you to give an entire answer to this my uncouth letter as to what and on what I may depend. But if it does not please you to answer me in writing, let me know some place where I may have it by word of mouth, and I will go thither with all my heart. No more for fear of annoying[1] you. Written by the hand of him who would willingly remain your

H Rex

---

[1] The *Harleian Miscellany* translates '*vous ennuyere*' as 'tiring you'. The word '*ennuyer*' is ambiguous here.

¹The *Harleian Miscellany* has 'a present' here – but Henry's word 'estrene' refers only to a New Year's gift. At Henry's court, the King and his favourites always exchanged gifts on New Year's Day.
²'Either here or nowhere'.
³The *Harleian Miscellany* omits this passage. Savage has 'bitterness', presumably misreading '*racine*' as '*rancune*'.
⁴Here Henry has incorporated his signature to convey the message that he seeks no other than Anne Boleyn: '*H aultre a.b. ne cherse Rex*'.

LETTER V

(Translated from the French. Probably written in the first days of January 1528.)

OR a New Year's gift[1] so beautiful that nothing could exceed it (considering the whole of it) I thank you most cordially, not only for the handsome diamond and ship in which the lonely damsel is tossed about, but chiefly for the fine interpretation and too humble submission which your goodness has made in this case; for I certainly think that it would be very difficult for me to deserve this, if it were not for your great humanity and favour. In this happiness I have tried, am trying, and will try to remain, by all means open to me; I hope this is my unchangeable intention, which is *Aut illic aut nullibi.*[2] The demonstrations of your affection are such, and the beautiful words of your letter are so cordially phrased, that they really oblige me to honour, love, and serve you for ever, imploring you to agree to continue in this same firm and constant purpose, assuring you that for my part I will out-do you, if this be possible, rather than reciprocate, in loyalty of heart and my desire to please you; and you, without any other ties[3] in your heart, can further this. Beseeching you also that if I have in any way offended you, you will give me the same absolution for which you ask, assuring you that henceforth my heart will be dedicated to you alone, and wishing greatly that my body was so too, for God can do it if He pleases; to whom I pray once a day for that end, hoping that at length my prayers will be heard. I wish the time may be short, but I shall think it long till we two meet again. Written by the hand of the secretary who in heart, body, and will is your loyal and most assured servant

H SEEKS A.B. NO OTHER REX[4]

King Henry at 30 by an unknown artist. The King bears a strong resemblance to his father Henry VII and to his elder brother Arthur.

Painting on a panel from the National Portrait Gallery, London.

LETTER VI

(Written in English, about 16 September 1528.)

HE reasonable request of your last letter, with the pleasure also that I take to know them true, causeth me to send you now these news. The legate[1] which we most desire arrived at Paris on Sunday or Monday last past; so that I trust, by the next Monday, to hear of his arrival at Calais; and then, I trust, within a while after, to enjoy that which I have so longed for, to God's pleasure and our both comforts. No more to you, at this present, mine own darling, for lack of time, but that I would you were in mine arms, or I in yours; for I think it long since I kissed you. Written after the killing of an hart, at xj[2] of the clock; minding with God's grace tomorrow mightily timely to kill another, by the hand of him which I trust shall shortly be yours

HENRY R.

[1]Cardinal Campeggio, the papal legate who had been sent to England to try Henry's divorce case against Catherine of Aragon.
[2]Henry, like nearly everyone else in sixteenth-century England, always wrote figures in Roman numerals. Eleven was always written 'xj'.

MATER ANNA REGINÆ BVLLEN REGINA ANGLIÆ ELIZABETHÆ

Nata Anᵒ 1507 Nupsit Anᵒ 1532 Nov 14
Eliz Filiam peperit Anᵒ 1533 Sept 7
Capite plexa Anᵒ 1536 May 19

Anne Boleyn captivated the King. In the last months of her marriage to Henry, the King, himself, complained that he had been bewitched by Anne. Yet she was described by a Venetian in the year of her marriage to Henry as 'not one of the handsomest women . . . she is of middling stature, swarthy complexion, long neck, wide mouth, bosom not much raised . . .' The diarist did admit, however, that her eyes were 'black and beautiful'.

Engraving of Anne Boleyn. Mary Evans Picture Library.

LETTER VII

(Written in English, about 20 August 1528.)

ARLING, though I have scant leisure, yet, remembering my promise, I thought it convenient to certify you briefly in what case our affairs stand. As touching a lodging for you, we have gotten one, by my Lord Cardinal's means, the like whereof could not have been found hereabouts for all causes, as this bearer shall more show you. As touching our other affairs, I ensure[1] you there can be no more done, nor more diligence used, nor all manner of dangers better both foreseen and provided for, so that I trust it shall be hereafter to both our comforts, the specialities whereof were both too long to be written and hardly by messenger to be declared. Wherefore till you repair hither, I keep that thing in store, trusting it shall not be long so. For I have caused my lord your father to make his provisions with speed. And thus, for lack of time, darling, I make an end of my letter, written with the hand of him which I would were yours,

H.R.

---

[1] Assure.

Probably painted in 1546 when she was thirteen, this is the earliest identifiable portrait of Princess Elizabeth, daughter of King Henry and Anne Boleyn. Her birth at Greenwich Palace weakened Anne Boleyn's position and was a severe blow to the King, who had been hoping desperately for a son. Henry was heard to compare Anne unfavourably with Catherine of Aragon and according to the Spanish ambassador Eustace Chapuys, the King told his wife that she should remember her lowly origins.

Elizabeth was later to say famously, at Tilbury in 1588 when faced with the Armada, 'I know I have the body of a weak and feeble woman: but I have the heart and stomach of a King, and a King of England too . . .'

Portrait from the Royal Collection.

LETTER VIII

(Translated from the French. Written before July 1527.)

THOUGH it is not fitting for a gentleman to take his lady in the place of a servant,[1] nevertheless, in complying with your wishes, I willingly grant them, so that you may be less displeased in the place that you yourself have chosen than you have been in that which I gave you. Thanking you most cordially that it pleases you still to have some remembrance of me. B.N.R.I. de R.O.M.V.E.Z.[2]

HENRY REX

[1] There has been disagreement as to the meaning of Henry's phrase *'Neanmoins quil nappatiente pas a ung gentylle homme pur prendre sa dame au lieu de servante'*, owing to the different possible meanings of *'au lieu'*. Savage suggests that, in the context of the letter, it should be translated 'Though it does not become a gentleman to visit his lady in the house of a servant' – but it should be noted that Henry wrote *'servante'* in the feminine, not the masculine *'serviteur'*, which he uses elsewhere.

[2] No one has succeeded in deciphering this code. The first initial, which I read as 'B', has been identified both as '6' and as 'O' – '6' is almost certainly wrong, for Henry would not have used an Arabic numeral.

The Maximilian Jewel was worn on the collar of the King's Order of the Garter. It was given to King Henry by Emperor Maximilian I. Maximilian died in 1519 and was succeeded by his grandson, the Emperor Charles, who championed the cause of his aunt Catherine of Aragon. It was Charles' support of Catherine's cause which prevented the Pope agreeing readily to the annulment of Catherine's marriage to King Henry.

From the Royal Collection.

LETTER IX

(Written in English, about 15 June 1528.)

HE cause of my writing at this time (good sweetheart) is only to understand of your good health and prosperity, whereof to know I would be as glad as in manner mine own, praying God that and it be His pleasure, to send us shortly together, for I promise you I long for it, howbeit trust it shall not be long too; and seeing my darling is absent, I can no less do than to send her some flesh representing my name, which is hart's flesh for Henry, prognosticating that hereafter, God willing, you must enjoy some of mine, which He pleased I would were now. As touching your sister's matter,[1] I have caused Walter Welshe to write to my lord mine mind therein, surely I trust that Eve shall not have power to deceive Adam. For surely, whatsoever is said, it cannot so stand with his honour but that he must needs take her his natural daughter now in her extreme necessity. No more to you at this time, mine own darling, but that with a wish I would we were together one evening with the hand of yours

H.R.

---

[1] This apparently refers to a dispute about property between Anne's sister, Mary, and their father, and to the illness of Mary's husband, Sir William Carey, who died from the sweating sickness on 22 June 1528.

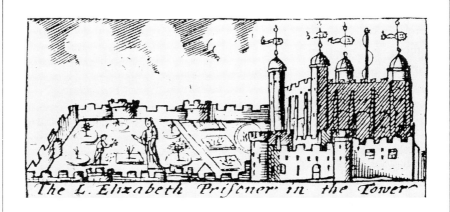

The L. Elizabeth Prisoner in the Tower

Princess Elizabeth as a prisoner in the Tower of London following Wyatt's unsuccessful rebellion. It was at the Tower that her mother was executed on her father's orders and buried without ceremony.

From a chap book.

LETTER X

(Translated from the French. Written before July 1527.)

LTHOUGH, my mistress, you have not been pleased to remember the promise which you made me when I was last with you, which was that I should hear good news of you and have an answer to my last letter; yet I think it is fitting for a true servant (since otherwise he can know nothing) to send to inquire about his mistress's welfare; and to acquit myself in the office of a true servant, I send you this letter, begging you to inform me that you are prospering, which I pray God you may continue to do, as I hope I will; and to make you think of me more often, I send you by this bearer a buck killed late last night by my hand, hoping that when you eat it, it will remind you of the hunter; and thus, for lack of space, I will make an end of my letter. Written by the hand of your servant, who often wishes you were in your brother's place.[1]

H REX

---

[1]Anne's brother, George, was an officer of the royal household, and in close attendance on the King.

app rochant du temps qui ma si longuement dure me rejoyst tante
qui me semble pres q De la Venus n ay au mains lentre accostumement ne
r perfra tant q le deux persons se assemblet la qlle assemble est plus desire
y moy endroyte que nulle chose mondayne car q rejoyssement peut estre
si grand en ce monde come daboyre la copanye de celle qui est le plus
there aymee sachant auss q uelle fait la pezzylle de son chose le penser qui
me fait grande pleasize pr Juger adoncques que fra le personage quillens
En q uelle ma fait plus grande mole au ceulz que m i tanpe mi escripture
peulet exprimere set que n ames aultre chose excepte ce la peut remedier
vous supliant ma mestzes de dire amonst vre pere de ma part que je
fuy pere de alumer de deux heures le temps assine qui peut estre en court
debent le vrell termeson au mains sur le avoir car q se pense
qu ll ne froyte point le toure de amonzeus qui disit m i accordant a
mon expectatioy non plus dastenre de faute de temps estre ant
bien toute que de boche vous diray la reste de parnnes pez
moy en vre absence sustennes escrypte de la main du sezetere
qui se sustait dastenre privrement opres de vous qui est et afume
. seraf

vre loyal et plus asure sedntenze

LETTER XI

(Translated from the French. Written about 21 July 1528.)

AM so looking forward to the approach of the time for which I have waited so long, that it seems to me that it has already nearly arrived;[1] but nevertheless the entire fulfilment cannot take place till the two persons meet, which meeting is more desired on my side than any worldly thing; for what joy can be greater in this world than to have the company of her who is my greatest friend, knowing too that she feels the same on her side? The thought of which gives me great pleasure. Judge, then, what effect she personally would have, whose absence has wounded my heart more than tongue or writing can express, and that nothing except this can remedy. Begging you, my mistress, to tell my lord your father from me that I wish him to bring forward by two days the appointed time, and to be at court before the old date, or at least by the day first chosen;[2] for otherwise I shall think that he is not serving the lovers' turn, as he said he would, nor fulfilling my expectations. No more now for lack of time, hoping soon to tell you by word of mouth the rest of my sufferings that I have endured in your absence. Written by the hand of the secretary who wishes that he were now with you privately, and who is, and always will be, your most loyal and assured servant

H   SEEKS A.B. NO OTHER   REX

[1] This seems to be the meaning of '*Lapprochant du temps qui ma si longement dure me rejoyet tante qui me semble pres que deja venu*'.
[2] This is the most likely meaning of '*je luy prie de avancer de deux jours le temps assine, qui peut estre en court devant le viell terme, ou aumoins sur le jour prefixe*'. To translate '*devant le viell terme*' as 'before the old [legal] term' would only make sense if it was 'before the end of the old term'. Henry was almost certainly referring to his royal court, not to a court of law.

Letter XII. Written in French, beginning 'There came suddenly to me in the night the most unpleasant news . . .'

From the Vatican Library, Rome.

LETTER XII

(Translated from the French. Written about 23 June 1528.)

HERE came suddenly to me in the night the most unpleasant news that I could have received, for I needs must grieve for three reasons. The first, because I heard of the illness of my mistress, who I esteem more than all the world, and would willingly bear half of your illness in order to have you cured. The second, because of my fear that I will be pressed even more by my enemy, Absence, which hitherto has caused me the greatest annoyance that he could, and, as far as I can judge, is planning to do worse. I pray God that He will rid me of so troublesome a rebel.[1] The third, because the physician in whom I most trust is absent at this moment when he could do me the greatest pleasure, because I hoped to obtain through him and his practices one of my greatest joys in this world, that is to say, to have my mistress cured. However, in default of him, I will send the second one, praying God that he will soon be able to make you well, and then I shall like him more than ever. I beseech you to be governed by his advice about your illness; if you do, I hope to see you again soon, which will be a greater cordial for me than all the precious stones in the world. Written by the secretary who is, and always will be, your loyal and most assured servant

H.　A.B.　R.

---

[1]The *Harleian Miscellany* translates Henry's '*rebell*' as 'tormentor', which hides the significant fact that Henry, with his belief in royal authority, should have chosen to describe his great enemy, Absence from Anne Boleyn, as a 'rebel'.

[1]The sweating sickness.
[2]On the death of the Abbess of Wilton, Wolsey wished to appoint her second-in-command, the Prioress of Wilton, Lady Isabel Jordan, to succeed her as Abbess – but Anne Boleyn wished to obtain this important and lucrative office for another of the nuns of Wilton, Dame Eleanor Carey, who was the sister-in-law of Anne's sister, Mary. When it was discovered that both the candidates for the office – and also a third possibility, Eleanor Carey's sister – had all been guilty of sexual immorality, Henry decided to choose another candidate as Abbess; but Wolsey refused to give way, and appointed the Prioress. This led to a quarrel between Henry and Wolsey.
[3]'Of yours only'.

LETTER XIII

(Written in English, about 7 July 1528.)

INCE your last letters, mine own darling, Walter Welche, Master Browne, John Carr, Yrion of Brearton, John Coke, the pothecary, be fallen of the sweat[1] in this house, and thanked be God all well recovered, so that as yet the plague is not fully ceased here; but I trust shortly it shall by the mercy of God; the rest of us yet be well, and I trust shall pass it, or not to have it or at least as easily as the rest have done. As touching the matter of Wilton,[2] my Lord Cardinal hath had the nuns before him, and examined them, Master Bell being present, which hath certified me that for a truth, that she hath confessed herself (which we would have had abbess) to have had two children by two sundry priests; and further, since hath been kept by a servant of the Lord Broke that was, and that not long ago. Wherefore I would not for all the gold in the world clog your conscience nor mine to make her ruler of a house which is of so ungodly demeanour; nor I trust you would not, that neither for brother nor sister I should so destain mine honour or conscience; and as touching the prioress, or Dame Eleanor's eldest sister, though there is not any evident case proved against them, and that the prioress is so old that of many years she could not be as she was named; yet notwithstanding, to do you pleasure, I have done that neither of them shall have it, but that some other and good and well disposed woman shall have it; whereby the house shall be the better reformed (whereof, I ensure you, it had much need) and God much the better served. As touching abode at Hever, do therein as best shall you like; for you know best what air doth best with you; but I would it were come thereto (if it pleased God) that neither of us need care for that, for I ensure you I think it long. Suche is fallen sick of the sweat, and therefore I send you this bearer, because I think you long to hear tidings from us, as we do in likewise from you. Written with the hand

De votre seul[3]

H.R.

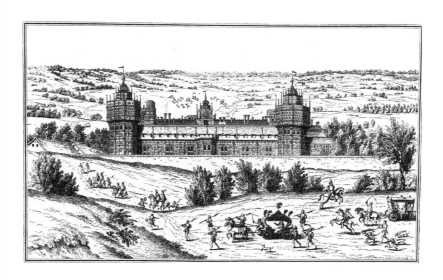

Nonsuch House was built in the last decade of Henry's reign, at the King's demand, to outdo the design of his rival King Francis' palace at Fontainebleau. A village, a church and a manor house were pulled down to clear the site for a house that was built for King Henry's 'solace and retirement'. Katherine Parr visited the house in 1544. But Catherine of Aragon's daughter Mary disliked the house and on her accession considered pulling it down. She was persuaded by the Earl of Arundel to exchange it with the Earl for lands in Suffolk.

The illustration, from a picture by Hofnegel, shows Anne Boleyn's daughter as Queen Elizabeth arriving at Nonsuch. In the last years of her reign, Elizabeth bought Nonsuch from Arundel's heir and the house became her favourite country seat. The house built but not completed by her father for his old age and disliked by her sister became, according to one of Elizabeth's courtiers, the house 'which of all places she likes best'.

From a picture by Hofnagel.

LETTER XIV

(Written in English, probably in February 1528.)

ARLING, these shall be only to advertise you that this bearer and his fellow[1] be dispatched with as many things to compass our matter, and to bring it to pass as our wits could imagine or devise; which brought to pass, as I trust by their diligence it shall be, shortly you and I shall have our desired end, which should be more to my heart's ease, and more quietness to my mind, than any other thing in this world, as with God's grace shortly I trust shall be proved, but not as soon as I would it were; yet I will ensure you there shall be no time lost that may be won, and further cannot be done, for *ultra posse non est esse.*[2] Keep him not too long with you, but desire him for your sake to make the more speed, for the sooner we have word from him, the sooner shall our matter come to pass; and thus, upon trust of your short repair to London, I make an end of my letter, mine own sweetheart. Written with the hand of him which desireth as much to be yours as you do to have him.

H.R.

[1]Stephen Gardiner (afterwards Bishop of Winchester) and Edward Fox (afterwards Bishop of Hereford).
[2]'Further it is impossible to be'.

Prince Edward as King Edward VI, King Henry's longed for and legitimate heir by Jane Seymour. In 1525, seven years before his divorce from Catherine of Aragon, King Henry took the desperate step of creating his illegitimate son by Elizabeth Blount, the Duke of Richmond and Somerset and giving him precedence over Princess Mary. Henry FitzRoy, Duke of Richmond, died in 1536, the year Henry married Jane Seymour.

Portrait from the Royal Collection.

LETTER XV

(Written in English, about 21 July 1528.)

ARLING, I heartily recommend me to you, ascertaining you that I am not a little perplexed with such things as your brother shall on my part declare unto you, to whom I pray you give full credence, for it were too long to write. In my last letters I wrote to you that I trusted shortly to see you, which is better known at London than with any that is about me, whereof I not a little marvel; but lack of discreet handling must needs be the cause thereof. No more to you at this time, but that I trust shortly our meetings shall not depend upon other men's light handlings, but upon your own. Written with the hand of him that longeth to be yours

H.R.

15.

Letter XVI. Written in English, beginning 'Mine own sweetheart . . .'
From the Vatican Library, Rome.

LETTER XVI

(Written in English, in July 1528.)

INE OWN SWEETHEART, these shall be to advertise you of the great elengeness[1] that I find here since your departing, for I ensure you, methinketh the time longer since your departing now last than I was wont to do a whole fortnight. I think your kindness and my fervence of love causeth it, for otherwise I would not have thought it possible that for so little a while it should have grieved me; but now that I am coming toward you, methinketh my pains been half released, and also I am right well comforted, insomuch that my book[2] maketh substantially for my matter, in writing whereof I have spent above iiij[3] hours this day, which caused me now to write the shorter letter to you at this time, because of some pain in my head, wishing myself (specially an evening) in my sweetheart's arms, whose pretty ducks[4] I trust shortly to kiss. Written with the hand of him that was, is, and shall be yours by his will

H.R.

---

[1]Loneliness.
[2]His book, *A Glasse of the Truthe*, in which he put forward theological arguments to prove that his marriage to Catherine of Aragon was against God's law, and void.
[3]In the sixteenth century, the number 'four' was always written in Roman numerals, 'iiij'.
[4]Breasts.

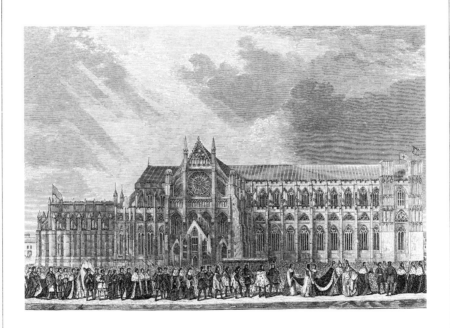

The coronation procession of Anne Boleyn took place on 1 June 1533. Her procession through the City of London was met by silence and sullenness from many of the resentful crowd. Parliament had passed an act to deny the Pope power to judge matrimonial cases arising in England. In May 1533 the newly consecrated Archbishop of Canterbury, Thomas Cranmer, had pronounced Henry's marriage to Catherine of Aragon void and his marriage to Anne Boleyn valid. The King married Anne, according to Cranmer, in early 1533, 'about 25 January'.

LETTER XVII

(Written in English, about 8 October 1528.)

o inform you what joy it is to me to understand of your comformableness with reason, and of the suppressing of your inutile[1] and vain thoughts and fantasies with the bridle of reason, I ensure you all the good in this world could not counterpoise for my satisfaction the knowledge and certainty thereof; wherefore, good sweetheart, continue the same not only in this, but in all your doings hereafter, for thereby shall come both to you and me the greatest quietness that may be in this world. The cause why this bearer tarrieth so long is the business that I have had to dress up gear for you, which I trust ere long to see you occupy; and then I trust to occupy yours, which shall be recompense enough for me for all my pains and labours. The unfeigned sickness of this well-willing legate[2] doth somewhat retard his access to your presence; but I trust verily, when God shall send him health, he will with diligence recompense his demur; for I know well where he hath said (lamenting the saying and bruit[3] that he should be thought imperial[4]) that it should be well known in this matter that he is not imperial. And thus for lack of time, farewell. Written with the hand which fain would be yours, and so is the heart.

H.R.

[1]Useless.
[2]Cardinal Campeggio was prevented by gout from transacting business for a fortnight after his arrival in London on 7 October 1528.
[3]Rumour.
[4]That he should be thought sympathetic to the Holy Roman Emperor, Charles the Fifth, who was supporting the cause of his aunt, Catherine of Aragon, and opposing Henry's divorce.

TWO LETTERS FROM ANNE BOLEYN TO CARDINAL WOLSEY

LETTER I

(Written about 17 June 1528.)

 Y LORD, in my most humble wise that my heart can think, I desire you to pardon me that I am so bold, to trouble you with my simple and rude writing, esteeming it to proceed from her, that is much desirous to know that your grace does well, as I perceive by this bearer that you do. The which I pray God long to continue, as I am most bound to pray; for I do know the great pains and troubles that you have taken for me, both day and night, is never like to be recompenced on my part, but alonely in loving you, next unto the king's grace, above all creatures living. And I do not doubt, but the daily proof of my deeds shall manifestly declare and affirm my writing to be true, and I do trust you do think the same. My lord, I do assure you, I do long to hear from you news of the legate; for I do hope, and they come from you, they shall be very good, and I am sure you desire it as much as I, and more, and it were possible, as I know it is not; and thus, remaining in a steadfast hope, I make an end of my letter, written with the hand of her that is most bound to be.

Postscript by King Henry

The writer of this letter would not cease till she had caused me likewise to set to my hand; desiring you, though it be short, to take it in good part. I ensure you, there is neither of us, but that greatly desireth to see you, and much more joyous to hear that you have scaped this plague so well, and trusting the fury thereof to be passed, specially with them that keepeth good diet, as I trust you do. The not hearing of the legate's arrival in France, causeth us somewhat to muse; notwithstanding, we trust your diligence and vigilancy (with the assistance of Almighty God) shortly to be eased out of that trouble. No more to you at this time; but that I pray God send you as good health prosperity, as the writer would.

By your loving sovereign and friend

HENRY R.

Your humble servant

ANNE BOLEYN

Thomas Cranmer, Archbishop of Canterbury, became Anne Boleyn's personal chaplain. He supported Henry in the King's 'Great Matter' of his divorce from Catherine, and thus against the Catholic Church. Cardinal Wolsey had also supported the King's divorce but his prevention of Anne's marriage to Lord Percy had earned him her hatred. He was charged with treason, perhaps at her instigation, and died in 1530 on his way to face trial.

Portrait of Cranmer by Flicke from the Portrait Gallery, London.

LETTER II

(Written about 7 July 1528.)

Y LORD, in my most humble wise that my poor heart can think, I do thank your grace for your kind letter, and for your rich and goodly present, the which I shall never be able to deserve without your help, of the which I have hitherto had so great plenty that, all the days of my life, I am most bound, of all creatures, next the king's grace, to love and serve your grace; of the which, I beseech you, never to doubt, that ever I shall vary from this thought as long as any breath is in my body. And, as touching your grace's trouble with the sweat, I thank our lord, that them I desired and prayed for are escaped, and that is the king and you; not doubting but that God has preserved you both for great causes known only to his high wisdom. And as for the coming of the legate, I desire that much; and, if it be God's pleasure, I pray him to send this matter shortly to a good end, and then I trust, my lord, to recompence part of your great pains. In the which, I must require you, in the mean time, to accept my good will in the stead of the power, the which must proceed partly from you, as our Lord knoweth; to whom I beseech to send you long life, with continuance in honour. Written with the hand of her that is most bound to be

Your humble and obedient servant

ANNE BOLEYN

ANNE BOLEYN'S LAST LETTER
TO KING HENRY

SIR

Your grace's displeasure, and my imprisonment, are things so strange unto me, as what to write, or what to excuse, I am altogether ignorant. Whereas you send unto me (willing me to confess a truth, and so to obtain your favour) by such an one whom you know to be mine ancient professed enemy; I no sooner received this message by him, than I rightly conceived your meaning; and if, as you say, Confessing a truth indeed may procure my safety, I shall with all willingness and duty perform your command.

But let not your grace ever imagine that your poor wife will ever be brought to acknowledge a fault, where not so much as a thought ever proceded. And to speak a truth, never a prince had wife more loyal in all duty, and in all true affection, than you have ever found in Ann Boleyn, with which name and place I could willingly have contented myself, if God and your grace's pleasure had been so pleased. Neither did I at any time so far forget myself in my exaltation, or received queenship, but that I always looked for such an alteration as now I find; for the ground of my preferment being on no surer foundation than your grace's fancy, the least alteration, I know, was fit and sufficient to draw that fancy to some other subject. You have chosen me from a low estate to be your queen and companion, far beyond my desert or desire. If then, you found me worthy of such honour, good your grace let not any light fancy, or bad counsel of mine enemies, withdraw your princely favour from me; neither let that stain, that unworthy stain of disloyal heart, towards your good grace, ever cast so foul a blot on your most dutiful wife, and the infant princess your daughter; try me, good king, but let me have a lawful trial, and let not my sworn enemies sit as my accusers and judges; yea, let me receive an open trial, for my truth shall fear no open shame; then shall you see, either mine innocency cleared, your suspicion and conscience satisfied, the ignominy and slander of the world stopped, or my guilt openly declared. So that, whatsoever God, or you may determine of me, your grace may be freed from an open censure; and mine offence being so lawfully proved, your grace is at liberty, both before God and man, not only to execute worthy punishment on me as an unlawful wife, but to follow your affection, already settled on that party, for whose sake I am now as I am, whose name I could some good while since have pointed unto; your grace being not ignorant of my suspicion therein.

But, if you have already determined of me, and that only my death, but an infamous slander must bring you the joying of your desired happiness; then I desire of God, that he will pardon your great sin herein, and likewise my enemies, the instruments thereof; and that he will not call you to a strait account for your unprincely and cruel usage of me, at his general judgment-seat, where both you and myself must shortly appear, and in whose judgment I doubt not (whatsoever the world may think of me), my innocence shall be openly known, and sufficiently cleared.

My last and only request shall be, that myself may only bear the burthen of your grace's displeasure, and that it may not touch the innocent souls of those poor gentlemen, whom, as I understand, are likewise in strait imprisonment for my sake. If ever I have found favour in your sight, if ever the name of Ann Boleyn hath been pleasing in your ears, let me obtain this request, and so I will leave to trouble your grace any further, with mine earnest prayer to the Trinity to have your grace in his good keeping, and to direct you in all your actions. From my doleful prison in the Tower, this sixth of May.

Your most loyal and ever faithful wife

Ann Boleyn

Jane Seymour was lady in waiting to Anne Boleyn. She, too, refused to become the King's mistress and insisted on becoming Queen, which she became although she was never crowned. She bore King Henry his long awaited legitimate son but died shortly afterwards from the effects of childbirth and fever. She is the only one of Henry's queens to share his tomb.

From the Maurits van Nassau Foundation, The Hague.

LETTER FROM KING HENRY VIII
TO JANE SEYMOUR

LETTER 1

(Written while Anne Boleyn was still his wife)

M Y DEAR FRIEND AND MISTRESS

The bearer of these few lines from thy entirely devoted servant will deliver into thy fair hands a token of my true affection for thee, hoping you will keep it for ever in your sincere love for me. Advertising you that there is a ballad made lately of great derision against us, which if it go much abroad and is seen by you, I pray you to pay no manner of regard to it. I am not at present informed who is the setter forth of this malignant writing but if he is found he shall be straitly punished for it. For the things ye lacked I have minded my lord to supply them to you as soon as he can buy them. This hoping shortly to receive you in these arms, I end for the present.

Your own loving servant and sovereign

H. R.

King Henry when he was about 45 years of age. This portrait was probably painted in 1536, the year in which Catherine of Aragon died and Anne Boleyn was executed. Catherine, her marriage to Henry annulled in England, was buried in Peterborough Abbey with the ceremony due to the widow of Arthur, prince of Wales. Anne was buried without ceremony in the Tower of London. The King married Jane Seymour ten days later.

Portrait from the National Portrait Gallery, London.

THE DEATH OF ANNE BOLEYN

In 1536 Anne miscarried of a son. Catherine of Aragon had died a few weeks before at Kimbolton Castle and Henry had long since tired of Anne's temper and contrariness. The qualities in her that had attracted the King and partly persuaded him to wait so long now irritated him and he had come to detest her. Only Anne stood between the King and a fresh and undoubtedly legitimate marriage. She was accused of incest with her brother Viscount Rochford and with having committed adultery with three courtiers and her lute player. She was tried and found guilty, as were her brother and her other alleged lovers.

On 17 May 1536, two days after her trial and two days before her death, Archbishop Cranmer declared her marriage to the King to be void. She was beheaded by a swordsman and buried with little ceremony at the Chapel of St Peter-ad-Vincula, in the Tower of London. Ten days later the King married Jane Seymour.

A cameo of King Henry VIII with his son Prince Edward who succeeded to the throne in 1547 at the age of nine.
From the Royal Collection.

PREVIOUS EDITIONS OF THE LETTERS

LOVE LETTERS FROM KING HENRY VIII TO ANNE BOLEYN. *Some in French and Some in English. To which are added Translations of Those Written in French. With an Appendix containing Two letters from Anne Boleyn to Cardinal Wolsey. With her last to Henry the VIIIth.* Printed by J. Churchill. London, 1714.

LETTERS OF KING HENRY VIII TO ANNE BOLEYN. In *Roberti de Avesbury Historia de Mirabilibus gestis Edwardi III.* Ed. T. Hearne. Oxford, 1720.

LOVE LETTERS FROM KING HENRY THE EIGHTH TO ANNE BOLEYN: *And two letters from Anne Boleyn to Cardinal Wolsey; with her Last to Henry the Eighth.* In the *Harleian Miscellany.* London, 1745.

THE LOVE LETTERS OF HENRY VIII TO ANNA BOLEYN. In *The Pamphleteer,* Volume 21. London, 1823.

LETTRES DE HENRI VIII à ANNE BOLEYN. Ed. G. A. Crapelet. Paris, 1826, reprinted 1835.

LETTERS AND PAPERS (FOREIGN AND DOMESTIC) OF THE REIGN OF KING HENRY VIII. Ed. J. Brewer and J. Gairdner, Volume IV. London, 1862–1920.

THE LOVE LETTERS OF HENRY VIII TO ANNE BOLEYN. Ed. J. O. Halliwell Phillips. London, 1907.

LOVE LETTERS OF HENRY VIII TO ANNE BOLEYN. Ed. L. Black. London, 1907, reprinted, 1933.

THE LETTERS OF KING HENRY VIII. Ed. M. St Clare Byrne. London, 1936.

THE LOVE LETTERS OF HENRY VIII. Ed. H. Savage. London, 1949.

INDEX